# INDEX

# BACK IN 2003

Military action is necessary to halt the spread of the ISIS "cancer," said President Obama. In his much anticipated address, he called for expanded airstrikes across Iraq and Syria, and new measures to arm and train Iraqi and Kurdish ground forces.

Missing from the chorus of outrage, however, has been any acknowledgement of the integral role of covert US and British regional military intelligence strategy in empowering and even directly sponsoring the very same virulent Islamist militants in Iraq, Syria and beyond, that went on to break away from al-Qaeda and form 'ISIS', the Islamic State of Iraq and Syria, or now simply, the Islamic State (IS).

Since 2003, Anglo-American power has secretly and openly coordinated direct and indirect support for Islamist terrorist groups linked to al-Qaeda across the Middle East and North Africa. This ill-conceived patchwork geo-strategy is a legacy of the persistent influence of neoconservative ideology, motivated by longstanding but often contradictory ambitions to dominate regional oil resources, defend an expansionist Israel, and in pursuit of these, re-draw the map of the Middle East.

Now despite Pentagon denials that there will be boots on the ground – and Obama's insistence that this would not be another "Iraq war" – local Kurdish military and intelligence sources confirm that US and German special operations forces are already "on the ground" here. US airstrikes on ISIS positions and arms supplies to the Kurds have also been accompanied by British RAF reconnaissance flights over the region and UK weapons shipments to Kurdish peshmerga forces.

Early during the 2003 invasion and occupation of Iraq, the US covertly supplied arms to al-Qaeda affiliated insurgents even while ostensibly supporting an emerging Shi'a-dominated administration.

Pakistani defense sources interviewed by Asia Times in February 2005 confirmed that insurgents described as "former Ba'ath party" loyalists – who were being recruited and trained by "al-Qaeda in Iraq" under the leadership of the late Abu Musab Zarqawi – were being supplied Pakistan-manufactured weapons by the US. The arms shipments included rifles, rocket-propelled grenade launchers, ammunition, rockets and other light weaponry.

These arms "could not be destined for the Iraqi security forces because US arms would be given to them", a source told Syed Saleem Shahzad – the Times' Pakistan bureau chief who, "known for his exposes of the Pakistani military" according to the New Yorker, was murdered in 2011. Rather, the US is playing a double-game to "head off" the threat of a "Shi'ite clergy-driven religious movement," said the Pakistani defense source. This was not the only way US strategy aided the rise of Zarqawi, a bin Laden mentee and brainchild of the extremist ideology that would later spawn 'ISIS.'

## Dividing Enemies

According to a little-known report *"Dividing Our Enemies"*, made by US Joint Special Operations University (JSOU), post-invasion Iraq was an interesting case study of fanning discontent among enemies, leading to 'red-against-red' [enemy-against-enemy] firefights. While counter-insurgency on the one hand requires US forces to ameliorate harsh or deprived living conditions of the indigenous populations to publicly win local hearts and minds.

In other words, US forces would pursue public legitimacy through conventional social welfare while simultaneously de-legitimizing local enemies by escalating intra-insurgent violence, knowing full-well that doing so will in turn escalate the number of innocent civilians *"caught in the crossfire."* The idea is that violence covertly calibrated by US special operations will not only weaken enemies through in-fighting but turn the population against them.

In this case, the 'enemy' consisted of jihadists, Ba'athists, and peaceful Sufis, who were in a majority but, like the militants, also opposed the US military presence and therefore needed to be influenced. The JSOU report referred to events in late 2004 in Fallujah where *"US psychological warfare (PSYOP) specialists"* undertook to *"set insurgents battling insurgents."*

This involved actually promoting Zarqawi's ideology, ironically, to defeat it: *"The PSYOP warriors crafted programs to exploit Zarqawi's murderous activities – and to disseminate them through meetings, radio and television broadcasts, handouts, newspaper stories, political cartoons, and posters – thereby diminishing his folk-hero image,"* and encouraging the different factions to pick each other off. *"By tapping into the Fallujans' revulsion and antagonism to the Zarqawi jihadis the Joint PSYOP Task Force did its 'best to foster a rift between Sunni groups.'"*

Yet as noted by Dahr Jamail, one of the few unembedded investigative reporters in Iraq after the war, the proliferation of propaganda linking the acceleration of suicide bombings to the persona of Zarqawi was not matched by meaningful evidence. His own search to substantiate the myriad claims attributing the insurgency to Zarqawi beyond anonymous US intelligence sources encountered only an *"eerie blankness"*.

The US military operation in Fallujah, largely justified on the claim that Zarqawi's militant forces had occupied the city, used white phosphorous, cluster bombs, and indiscriminate air strikes to pulverize 36,000 of Fallujah's 50,000 homes, killing nearly a thousand civilians, terrorizing 300,000 inhabitants to flee, and culminating in a disproportionate increase in birth defects, cancer and infant mortality due to the devastating environmental consequences of the war.

To this day, Fallujah has suffered from being largely cut-off from wider Iraq, its infrastructure largely unworkable with water and sewage systems still in disrepair, and its citizens subject to sectarian discrimination and persecution by Iraqi government backed Shi'a militia and police. *"Thousands of bereaved and homeless Falluja families have a new reason to hate the US and its allies,"* observed The Guardian in 2005. Thus, did the US occupation plant the seeds from which Zarqawi's legacy would coalesce into the Frankenstein monster that calls itself "the Islamic State."

## Camp Bucca

Beyond conspiracy theories – which are often justified in an era where everything appears as though it is part of a plan or a scheme – we have the right to ask why the majority of the leaders of the Islamic State (IS), formerly the Islamic State in Iraq and Syria (ISIS), had all been incarcerated in the same prison at Camp Bucca, which was run by the US occupation forces near Omm Qasr in southeastern Iraq.

In the context of conspiracy theories, there are a lot of rumors about links between IS and the US intelligence or affiliated organizations. But to what extent are these theories credible? Is there evidence that corroborate them?

These questions seem legitimate, provided that ready-made answers are not accepted without convincing evidence. However, it is difficult to get this kind of evidence, and we might need another Edward Snowden or WikiLeaks to learn the real truth about the relationship between IS and US intelligence.

Yet not having this evidence should not prevent us from trying to gather some clues that may not amount to definitive evidence, but which will no doubt question the narrative that fully exonerates US intelligence from involvement with the jihadis.

First of all, most IS leaders had passed through the former U.S. detention facility at Camp Bucca in Iraq. So who were the most prominent of these detainees?

Abu Ayman al-Iraqi… also "graduated" from Camp Bucca, and currently serves as a member on IS' military council. The leader of IS, Abu Bakr al-Baghdadi, tops the list. He was detained from 2004 until mid-2006. After he was released, he formed the Army of Sunnis, which later merged with the so-called Mujahideen Shura Council.

What happened during Baghdadi's detention in Bucca remains a mystery. Some press reports said he had been detained as a "civilian" in prison for 10 months in 2004, while other reports stated he was captured by the US forces in 2005 and held for four years at Camp Bucca. This latter possibility is unlikely, given that Baghdadi had formed the Army of Sunnis and joined the Mujahideen Shura Council shortly before the assassination of Abu Musab al-Zarqawi in June 2006. This is while bearing in mind that this council was established in January 2006, which makes it more likely that Baghdadi had been released either in late 2005 or early 2006.

It should be noted that after the Army of the Sunnis merged with the Mujahideen Shura Council, the Americans were able to successfully hunt down the leaders of al-Qaeda in Iraq, starting with Zarqawi in 2006, and not ending with Abu Omar al-Baghdadi and Abu Hamza al-

Muhajir in 2010, the death of the former being the event that paved the way for Abu Bakr al-Baghdadi to become the organization's leader.

Another prominent IS leader today is Abu Ayman al-Iraqi, who was a former officer in the Iraqi army under Saddam Hussein. This man also "graduated" from Camp Bucca, and currently serves as a member on IS' military council.

Another member of the military council who was in Bucca is Adnan Ismail Najm. He was known as Osama al-Bilawi (Abu Abdul_Rahman al-Bilawi). IS named the operation for the "invasion of Mosul" after him. He was detained on January 2005 in Bucca, and was also a former officer in Saddam's army. He was the head of a shura council in IS, before he was killed by the Iraqi army near Mosul on June 4, 2014.

Camp Bucca was also home to Haji Samir, aka Haji Bakr, whose real name is Samir Abed Hamad al-Obeidi al-Dulaimi. He was a colonel in the army of the former Iraqi regime. He was detained in Bucca, and after his release, he joined al-Qaeda. He was the top man in ISIS in Syria, but was killed in Aleppo in the first week of January 2014.

According to the testimonies of US officers who worked in the prison, the administration of Camp Bucca had taken measures including the segregation of prisoners on the basis of their ideology. This, according to experts, made it possible to recruit people directly and indirectly. Former detainees had said in documented television interviews that Bucca, which was closed down in September 2009, was akin to an "al-Qaeda school."

Former detainees had said in documented television interviews that Bucca, which was closed down in September 2009, was akin to an "al-Qaeda school," where senior extremist gave lessons on explosives and suicide attacks to younger prisoners. A former prisoner named Adel Jassem Mohammed said that one of the extremists remained in the prison for two weeks only, but even so was able to recruit 25 out of 34 inmates who were there. Mohammed also said that U.S. military officials did nothing to stop the extremists from mentoring the other detainees.

While Camp Bucca is the common denominator among most IS leaders, another one is the fact that a majority of them were officers in the Baathist army, which explains the ease with which the radical group has been able to infiltrate the clans and coax some of their leaders into joining its ranks.

Another noteworthy point is that none of the leaders who had emerged out of Bucca and who were subsequently killed, were killed in U.S. airstrikes, but rather at the hands of the Iraqi army, the Syrian army, or in fighting with other armed groups.

What had happened in Bucca then? What were the circumstances that made all those former detainees subsequent leaders in the extremist group? These questions require answers and serious investigations. No doubt, we will one day discover that many more leaders in the group had been detained in Bucca as well, which seems to have been more of a "terrorist academy" than a prison.

# SYRIA's DIRTY WAR

## UK's covert action in Syria

According to former French foreign minister Roland Dumas, Britain had planned covert action in Syria as early as 2009: *"I was in England two years before the violence in Syria on other business,"* he told French television. *"I met with top British officials, who confessed to me that they were preparing something in Syria. This was in Britain not in America. Britain was preparing gunmen to invade Syria."*

Leaked emails from the private intelligence firm *Stratfor*, including notes from a meeting with Pentagon officials, confirmed that as of 2011, US and UK special forces training of Syrian opposition forces was well underway. The goal was to elicit the "collapse" of Assad's regime "from within."

Since then, the role of the Gulf states – namely Saudi Arabia, Qatar, Kuwait, the United Arab Emirates, and Jordan (as well as NATO member Turkey) – in officially and unofficially financing and coordinating the most virulent elements amongst Syria's rebels under the tutelage of US military intelligence is no secret. Yet the conventional wisdom is that the funneling of support to Islamist extremists in the rebel movement affiliated to al-Qaeda has been a colossal and regrettable error.

The reality is very different. The empowerment of the Islamist factions within the 'Free Syrian Army' (FSA) was a foregone conclusion of the strategy.

## Libya's experience

In its drive to depose Col. Qaddafi in Libya, NATO had previously allied itself with rebels affiliated to the al-Qaeda faction, the *Islamic Fighting Group*. The resulting Libyan regime backed by the US was in turn liaising with FSA leaders in Istanbul to provide money and heavy weapons for the anti-Assad insurgency. The State Department even hired an al-Qaeda affiliated Libyan militia group to provide security for the US embassy in Benghazi – although they had links with the very people that attacked the embassy.

## West training rebels

With their command and control center based in Istanbul, Turkey, military supplies from Saudi Arabia and Qatar in particular were transported by Turkish intelligence to the border for rebel acquisition. CIA operatives along with Israeli and Jordanian commandos were also training FSA rebels on the Jordanian-Syrian border with anti-tank and anti-aircraft weapons.

In addition, other reports show that British and French military were also involved in these secret training programs. It appears that the same FSA rebels receiving this elite training went straight into ISIS – one ISIS commander, Abu Yusaf, said, "Many of the FSA people who the west has trained are actually joining us."

*The National* thus confirmed the existence of another Command and Control Center in Amman, Jordan, "*staffed by western and Arab military officials,*" which "*channels vehicles, sniper rifles, mortars, heavy machine guns, small arms and ammunition to Free Syrian Army units.*" Rebel and opposition sources described the weapons bridge as "*a well-run operation staffed by high-ranking military officials from 14 countries, including the US, European nations and Arabian Gulf states, the latter providing the bulk of materiel and financial support to rebel factions.*"

The FSA sources interviewed by *The National* went to pains to deny that any al-Qaeda affiliated factions were involved in the control center, or would receive any weapons support. But this is difficult to believe given that "*Saudi and Qatari-supplied weapons*" were being funneled through to the rebels via Amman, to their favored factions.

Classified assessments of the military assistance supplied by US allies Saudi Arabia and Qatar obtained by the New York Times showed that "*most of the arms shipped at the behest of Saudi Arabia and Qatar to supply Syrian rebel groups… are going to hardline Islamic jihadists, and not the more secular opposition groups that the West wants to bolster.*"

Lest there be any doubt as to the extent to which all this covert military assistance coordinated by the US has gone to support al-Qaeda affiliated factions in the FSA, it is worth noting that earlier this year, the Israeli military intelligence website Debkafile – run by two veteran correspondents who covered the Middle East for 23 years for The Economist – reported that: "*Turkey is giving Syrian rebel forces, including the al-Qaeda-affiliated Nusra Front, passage through its territory to attack the northwestern Syrian coastal area around Latakia.*"

In August, Debkafile reported that "*The US, Jordan and Israel are quietly backing the mixed bag of some 30 Syrian rebel factions*", some of which had just "*seized control of the Syrian side of the Quneitra crossing, the only transit point between Israeli and Syrian Golan.*" However, Debkafile noted, "*al-Qaeda elements have permeated all those factions.*" Israel has provided limited support to these rebels in the form of "*medical care,*" as well as "*arms, intelligence and food*".

# ISIS sponsors

The Islamic State of Iraq and Syria (ISIS), now threatening Baghdad, was funded for years by wealthy donors in Kuwait, Qatar, and Saudi Arabia, three U.S. allies that have dual agendas in the war on terror.

It's an ironic twist, especially for donors in Kuwait (who, to be fair, back a wide variety of militias). ISIS has aligned itself with remnants of the Baathist regime once led by Saddam Hussein. Back in 1990, the U.S. attacked Iraq in order to liberate Kuwait from Hussein's clutches. Now Kuwait is helping the rise of his successors.

As ISIS takes over town after town in Iraq, they are acquiring money and supplies including American made vehicles, arms, and ammunition. The group reportedly scored $430 million when they looted the main bank in Mosul. They reportedly now have a stream of steady income sources, including from selling oil in the Northern Syrian regions they control, sometimes directly to the Assad regime.

But in the years they were getting started, a key component of ISIS's support came from wealthy individuals in the Arab Gulf States of Kuwait, Qatar and Saudi Arabia. Sometimes the support came with the tacit nod of approval from those regimes; often, it took advantage of poor money laundering protections in those states, according to officials, experts, and leaders of the Syrian opposition, which is fighting ISIS as well as the regime.

*"Everybody knows the money is going through Kuwait and that it's coming from the Arab Gulf,"* said Andrew Tabler, senior fellow at the Washington Institute for Near East Policy. *"Kuwait's banking system and its money changers have long been a huge problem because they are a major conduit for money to extremist groups in Syria and now Iraq."*

Iraqi Prime Minister Nouri al-Maliki has been publicly accusing Saudi Arabia and Qatar of funding ISIS for months. Several reports have detailed how private Gulf funding to various Syrian rebel groups has splintered the Syrian opposition and paved the way for the rise of groups like ISIS and others

Gulf donors support ISIS, the Syrian branch of al Qaeda called *al Nusrah Front*, and other Islamic groups fighting on the ground in Syria because they feel an obligation to protect Sunnis suffering under the atrocities of the Assad regime. Many of these backers don't trust or like the American backed moderate opposition, which the West has refused to provide significant arms to.

Under significant U.S. pressure, the Arab Gulf governments have belatedly been cracking down on funding to Sunni extremist groups, but Gulf regimes are also under domestic pressure to fight in what many Sunnis see as an unavoidable Shiite-Sunni regional war that is only getting worse by the day.

*"ISIS is part of the Sunni forces that are fighting Shia forces in this regional sectarian conflict. They are in an existential battle with both the (Iranian aligned) Maliki government and the Assad regime,"* said Tabler. *"The U.S. has made the case as strongly as they can to regional countries, including Kuwait. But ultimately when you take hands off, leading from behind approach to things, people don't take you seriously and they take matters into their own hands."*

Donors in Kuwait, the Sunni majority Kingdom on Iraq's border, have taken advantage of Kuwait's weak financial rules to channel hundreds of millions of dollars to a host of Syrian rebel brigades, according to a December 2013 report by The Brookings Institution, a Washington think tank that receives some funding from the Qatari government.

*"Over the last two and a half years, Kuwait has emerged as a financing and organizational hub for charities and individuals supporting Syria's myriad rebel groups,"* the report said. *"Today, there is evidence that Kuwaiti donors have backed rebels who have committed atrocities and who are either directly linked to al-Qa'ida or cooperate with its affiliated brigades on the ground."*

Kuwaiti donors collect funds from donors in other Arab Gulf countries and the money often travels through Turkey or Jordan before reaching its Syrian destination, the report said. The governments of Kuwait, Qatar, and Saudi Arabia have passed laws to curb the flow of illicit funds, but many donors still operate out in the open. The Brookings paper argues the U.S. government needs to do more.

*"The U.S. Treasury is aware of this activity and has expressed concern about this flow of private financing. But Western diplomats' and officials' general response has been a collective shrug,"* the report states.

When confronted with the problem, Gulf leaders often justify allowing their Salafi constituents to fund Syrian extremist groups by pointing back to what they see as a failed U.S. policy in Syria and a loss of credibility after President Obama reneged on his pledge to strike Assad after the regime used chemical weapons.

That's what Prince Bandar bin Sultan, head of Saudi intelligence since 2012 and former Saudi ambassador in Washington, reportedly told Secretary of State John Kerry when Kerry pressed him on Saudi financing of extremist groups earlier this year. Saudi Arabia has retaken a leadership role in past months guiding help to the Syrian armed rebels, displacing Qatar, which was seen as supporting some of the worst organizations on the ground.

The rise of ISIS, a group that officially broke with al Qaeda core, is devastating for the moderate Syrian opposition, which is now fighting a war on two fronts, severely outmanned and outgunned by both extremist groups and the regime. There is increasing evidence that Assad is working with ISIS to squash the Free Syrian Army.

But the Syrian moderate opposition is also wary of confronting the Arab Gulf states about their support for extremist groups. The rebels are still competing for those governments' favor and they are dependent on other types of support from Arab Gulf countries. So instead, they blame others—the regimes in Tehran and Damascus, for examples—for ISIS' rise.

*"The Iraqi State of Iraq and the [Sham] received support from Iran and the Syrian intelligence,"* said Hassan Hachimi, Head of Political Affairs for the United States and Canada for Syrian National Coalition, at the Brookings U.S.-Islamic World Forum in Doha this week.

*"There are private individuals in the Gulf that do support extremist groups there,"* along with other funding sources, countered Mouaz Moustafa, executive director of the Syrian Emergency Task Force, a Syrian-American organization that supports the opposition *"[The extremist groups] are the most well-resourced on the ground... If the United States and the international community better resourced [moderate] battalions... then many of the people will take that option instead of the other one."*

## US aid

Officially, the US government's financial support for the FSA goes through the Washington DC entity, the *Syrian Support Group* (SSG), which was incorporated in April 2012. The SSG is licensed via the US Treasury Department to *"export, re-export, sell, or supply to the Free Syrian Army ('FSA') financial, communications, logistical, and other services otherwise prohibited by Executive Order 13582 in order to support the FSA."*

In mid-2013, the Obama administration intensified its support to the rebels with a new classified executive order reversing its previous policy limiting US direct support to only nonlethal equipment. As before, the order would aim to supply weapons strictly to "moderate" forces in the FSA.

US government had *"little oversight over whether US supplies are falling prey to corruption – or into the hands of extremists,"* and relies *"on too much good faith."* The US government kept track of rebels receiving assistance purely through *"handwritten receipts provided by rebel commanders in the field,"* and the judgement of its allies. Countries supporting the rebels – the very same which have empowered al-Qaeda affiliated Islamists – *"are doing audits of the delivery of lethal and nonlethal supplies."*

Thus, with the Gulf states still calling the shots on the ground, it is no surprise that by September last year, eleven prominent rebel groups distanced themselves from the 'moderate' opposition leadership and allied themselves with al-Qaeda.

By the SSG's own conservative estimate, as much as 15% of rebel fighters are Islamists affiliated to al-Qaeda, either through the Jabhut al-Nusra faction, or its breakaway group ISIS. But privately, Pentagon officials estimate that *"more than 50%"* of the FSA is comprised of Islamist extremists, and according to rebel sources neither FSA chief Gen Salim Idris nor his senior aides engage in much vetting, decisions about which are made typically by local commanders.

# Follow the money

Media reports following ISIS' conquest of much of northern and central Iraq have painted the group as the world's most super-efficient, self-financed, terrorist organization that has been able to consolidate itself exclusively through extensive looting of Iraq's banks and funds from black market oil sales. Much of this narrative, however, has derived from dubious sources, and overlooked disturbing details.

One senior anonymous intelligence source told Guardian, for instance, that over 160 computer flash sticks obtained from an ISIS hideout revealed information on ISIS' finances that was completely new to the intelligence community. *"Before Mosul, their total cash and assets were $875m [£515m],"* said the official on the funds obtained largely via *"massive cash flows from the oil fields of eastern Syria, which it had commandeered in late 2012."*

Afterwards, *"with the money they robbed from banks and the value of the military supplies they looted, they could add another $1.5bn to that."* The thrust of the narrative coming from intelligence sources was simple: *"They had done this all themselves. There was no state actor at all behind them, which we had long known. They don't need one."*

# Follow the oil

But while ISIS has clearly obtained funding from donors in the Gulf states, many of its fighters having broken away from the more traditional al-Qaeda affiliated groups like Jabhut al-Nusra, it has also successfully leveraged its control over Syrian and Iraqi oil fields.

New York Times reported that *"Islamist rebels and extremist groups have seized control of most of Syria's oil and gas resources"*, bolstering *"the fortunes of the Islamic State of Iraq and Syria, or ISIS, and the Nusra Front, both of which are offshoots of al-Qaeda."* Al-Qaeda affiliated rebels had *"seized control of the oil and gas fields scattered across the country's north and east,"* while more moderate *"Western-backed rebel groups do not appear to be involved in the oil trade, in large part because they have not taken over any oil fields."*

In April 2013, for instance, the Times noted that al-Qaeda rebels had taken over key regions of Syria: *"Nusra's hand is felt most strongly in Aleppo"*, where the al-Qaeda affiliate had established in coordination with other rebel groups including ISIS *"a Shariah Commission"* running *"a police force and an Islamic court that hands down sentences that have included lashings."* Al-Qaeda fighters also *"control the power plant and distribute flour to keep the city's bakeries running."*

Additionally, they *"have seized government oil fields"* in provinces of Deir al-Zour and Hasaka, and now make a *"profit from the crude they produce."*

Lost in the fog of media hype was the disconcerting fact that these al-Qaeda rebel bread and oil operations in Aleppo, Deir al-Zour and Hasaka were directly and indirectly supported by the US and the European Union (EU). One account by the Washington Post for instance refers to a stealth mission in Aleppo *"to deliver food and other aid to needy Syrians – all of it paid for by the US government,"* including the supply of flour. *"The bakery is fully supplied with flour paid for by the United States,"* the Post continues, noting that local consumers, however, *"credited Jabhat al-Nusra – a rebel group the United States has designated a terrorist organisation because of its ties to al-Qaeda – with providing flour to the region, though he admitted he wasn't sure where it comes from."*

And in the same month that al-Qaeda's control of Syria's main oil regions in Deir al-Zour and Hasaka was confirmed, the EU voted to ease an oil embargo on Syria to allow oil to be sold on international markets from these very al-Qaeda controlled oil fields. European companies would be permitted to buy crude oil and petroleum products from these areas, although transactions would be approved by the Syrian National Coalition. Due to damaged infrastructure, oil would be trucked by road to Turkey where the nearest refineries are located.

## Turkey's dirty game

Even as al-Qaeda fighters increasingly decide to join up with IS, the ad hoc black market oil production and export infrastructure established by the Islamist groups in Syria has continued to function with, it seems, the tacit support of regional and western powers.

According to Ali Ediboglu, a Turkish MP for the border province of Hatay, IS is selling the bulk of its oil from regions in Syria and Mosul in Iraq through Turkey, with the tacit consent of Turkish authorities: *"They have laid pipes from villages near the Turkish border at Hatay. Similar pipes exist also at [the Turkish border regions of] Kilis, Urfa and Gaziantep. They transfer the oil to Turkey and parlay it into cash. They take the oil from the refineries at zero cost. Using primitive means, they refine the oil in areas close to the Turkish border and then sell it via Turkey. This is worth $800 million."* He also noted that the extent of this and related operations indicates official Turkish complicity. *"Fighters from Europe, Russia, Asian countries and Chechnya are going in large numbers both to Syria and Iraq, crossing from Turkish territory. There is information that at least 1,000 Turkish nationals are helping those foreign fighters sneak into Syria and Iraq to join ISIS. The National Intelligence Organization (MIT) is allegedly involved. None of this can be happening without MIT's knowledge."*

Similarly, there is evidence that authorities in the Kurdish region of Iraq are also turning a blind eye to IS oil smuggling. In July, Iraqi officials said that IS had begun selling oil extracted from in the northern province of Salahuddin. One official pointed out that "the Kurdish peshmerga forces stopped the sale of oil at first, but later allowed tankers to transfer and sell oil."

State of Law coalition MP Alia Nasseef also accused the Kurdistan Regional Government (KRG) of secretly trading oil with IS: *"What is happening shows the extent of the massive conspiracy against Iraq by Kurdish politicians... The [illegal] sale of Iraqi oil to ISIS or anyone else is something that would not surprise us."* Although Kurdish officials have roundly rejected these accusations, informed sources told the Arabic daily Asharq Al-Awsat that Iraqi crude captured by ISIS was *"being sold to Kurdish traders in the border regions straddling Iraq, Iran and Syria, and was being shipped to Pakistan where it was being sold 'for less than half its original price.'"*

*"Countries like Turkey have turned a blind eye to the practice"* of IS oil smuggling, said Luay al-Khateeb, a fellow at the Brookings Doha Center, *"and international pressure should be mounted to close down black markets in its southern region."* So far there has been no such pressure. Meanwhile, IS oil smuggling continues, with observers inside and outside Turkey noting that the Turkish government is tacitly allowing IS to flourish as it prefers the rebels to the Assad regime.

According to former Iraqi oil minister Isam al-Jalabi, *"Turkey is the biggest winner from the Islamic State's oil smuggling trade."* Both traders and oil firms are involved, he said, with the low prices allowing for "massive" profits for the countries facilitating the smuggling.

## Buying ISIS oil?

Early last month, a tanker carrying over a million barrels in crude oil from northern Iraq's Kurdish region arrived at the Texas Gulf of Mexico. The oil had been refined in the Iraqi Kurdish region before being pumped through a new pipeline from the KRG area ending up at Ceyhan, Turkey, where it was then loaded onto the tanker for shipping to the US. Baghdad's efforts to stop the oil sale on the basis of its having national jurisdiction were rebuffed by American courts.

In early September, the European Union's ambassador to Iraq, Jana Hybášková, told the EU Foreign Affairs Committee that *"several EU member states have bought oil from the Islamic State (IS, formerly ISIS) terrorist organisation that has been brutally conquering large portions of Iraq and Syria,"* according to Israel National News. She however *"refused to divulge the names of the countries despite being asked numerous times."*

A third end-point for the KRG's crude, once again shipped via Turkey's port of Ceyhan, was Israel's southwestern port of Ashkelon. This is hardly news though. In May, Reuters revealed that Israeli and US oil refineries had been regularly purchasing and importing KRG's disputed oil.

Meanwhile, as this triangle of covert oil shipments in which ISIS crude appears to be hopelessly entangled becomes more established, Turkey has increasingly demanded that the US pursue formal measures to lift obstacles to Kurdish oil sales to global markets. The KRG plans to export as much as 1 million barrels of oil a day by next year through its pipeline to Turkey.

Among the many oil and gas firms active in the KRG capital, Erbil, are ExxonMobil and Chevron. They are drilling in the region for oil under KRG contracts, though operations have been halted due to the crisis. No wonder Steve Coll writes in the New Yorker that Obama's air strikes and arms supplies to the Kurds – notably not to Baghdad – effectively amount to *"the defense of an undeclared Kurdish oil state whose sources of geopolitical appeal – as a long-term, non-Russian supplier of oil and gas to Europe, for example – are best not spoken of in polite or naïve company."* The Kurds are now busy working to "quadruple" their export capacity, while US policy has increasingly shifted toward permitting Kurdish exports – a development that would have major ramifications for Iraq's national territorial integrity.

To be sure, as the offensive against IS ramps up, the Kurds are now selectively cracking down on IS smuggling efforts – but the measures are too little, too late.

## The silence of the media

As ISIS went public with its expansion into Iraq followed by a succession of reports about its takeover of Iraqi cities and towns, in parallel with mass executions against civilians, the Western media was stunned. Several editorials raised questions about ISIS' funding and support. On June 13, officials at the US Treasury Department said Saudi Arabia was "on the same wavelength" as the United States, with both sides agreeing on the need to put an end to the radical group's operations.

In June as well, Lori Plotkin Boghardt of the Washington Institute for Near East Policy, wrote, "At present, there is no credible evidence that the Saudi government is financially supporting ISIS. Riyadh views the group as a terrorist organization that poses a direct threat to the kingdom's security." She continued, "Many governments in the region and beyond sometimes fund inimical parties to help achieve particular policy objectives. Riyadh has taken pleasure in recent ISIS-led Sunni advances against Iraq's Shia government, and in jihadist gains in Syria at Bashar al-Assad's expense."

Boghardt added, "Today, Saudi citizens continue to represent a significant funding source for Sunni groups operating in Syria. Arab Gulf donors as a whole – of which Saudis are believed to be the most charitable – have funneled hundreds of millions of dollars to Syria in recent years, including to ISIS and other groups."

At around the same time, Boghardt's colleague at the Washington Institute Andrew Tabler said candidly, "Everybody knows the money is going through Kuwait and that it's coming from the Arab Gulf. Kuwait's banking system and its money changers have long been a huge problem because they are a major conduit for money to extremist groups in Syria and now Iraq."

In addition to the issue of funding, the tone of some articles as concerns Saudi Arabia specifically changed over the recent period. Some analysts went back to the US ties to Osama bin Laden's al-Qaeda in the 1980s in Afghanistan, while others called on Saudi Arabia, Qatar, Gulf nations, and Turkey to put an end to their involvement immediately.

Some journalists and writers in the mainstream Western media finally broke their silence. Headlines were saying it more candidly now: Saudis must stop exporting extremism. Some journalists and writers in the mainstream Western media finally broke their silence. Headlines were saying it more candidly now: Saudis must stop exporting extremism, as an editorial by Ed Husain declared in NYT a few weeks ago. Husain wrote, "ISIS atrocities started with Saudi support for Salafi hate." Husain said that it was not enough for Saudi to give $100 million to the UN fund for counterterrorism, but that it must stop supporting all extremist Salafi groups around the world, and stop promoting extremist Salafi ideas and teachings among Saudis and Muslims elsewhere.

The writer, who had declared himself to be a Sunni Muslim at a meeting organized by the U.S. Council on Foreign Relations, explained at length the danger the Wahhabi ideology poses to the region and the world, saying, *"I'd say the Iranians haven't been as vociferous. Yes, they've funded Hezbollah and, yes, they've funded the Assad government, but neither have the level of dislike and hatred of Sunnis that the Saudis have pumped into their institutions, their syllabi in various mosques and madrassas that they control that has led to real hatred of Shia Muslims from Pakistan to the Caucasus to parts of Africa to Afghanistan to mostly in the Middle East."*

For its part, *The Washington Post* recently decided to re-highlight the issue of human rights violations in the kingdom, in a front-page editorial rather than in the international section. Meanwhile, WP contributor David Ignatius, who is close to Saudi's allies in the region, recalled in a recent article Bandar's "unpredictable" policies in Syria. Ignatius conveyed timidly accusations against the Saudi prince of having supported al-Qaeda-affiliated groups in Syria "unintentionally." He wrote, *"U.S. officials were relieved when Bandar was removed as steward of the Syrian opposition."* Ignatius also described Bandar as an "untrustworthy operator," as per the view held by some US officials, and as "flamboyant" and a Saudi "wild card."

Last month, *The Atlantic* quoted a senior Qatari official as saying that ISIS was a Saudi project. The magazine also said that the radical jihadi group was an essential part of Bandar's covert strategy in Syria.

Patrick Cockburn in the British newspaper The Independent quoted the former head of the British Secret Intelligence Service, MI6, Sir Richard Dearlove, who in turn was quoting what Bandar told him personally shortly before 9/11, as saying, "The time is not far off in the Middle East, Richard, when it will be literally 'God help the Shia'." Dearlove pointed out that the Saudi and Qatari regimes had turned a blind eye to the funds being sent to ISIS, and explained that ISIS's takeover of areas in Iraq and the extent at which the group had grown could not have happened "spontaneously." Dearlove said what Bandar had told him and subsequent events in the region were "chilling."

# SAUDI INTEL MASTERS

## The Coalition of hypocrisy

The Islamic State (ISIS) did not become the monster it is today by accident. The Western media and governments bore witness to the inception, growth, and expansion of this radical jihadi group, with funding from the Arab Gulf, sectarian agitation, and political blessing, until ISIS became a monster.

When the Saudi king charged Bandar bin Sultan with handling the Syrian file, as the latter was appointed chief of Saudi intelligence in 2012, Western analysts saw the move as an indication that Saudi Arabia was stepping up its involvement in Syria and of its intention to play a greater role there. But what role could that have been? No one identified the nature or type of this escalation.

*"Thank God for the Saudis and Prince Bandar, we're starting to see a little bit of reversal there [in Syria],"* said Republican Senator John McCain to CNN. The senator restated his gratitude at a security conference in Munich later, with a new twist. He said, *"Thank God for the Saudis, Prince Bandar, and our Qatari friends."*

Between 2013 and February 2014 – that is, throughout Prince Bandar's handling of the Syrian file – press reports covered extensively the rise of al-Nusra Front and ISIS in Syria, and how they became the dominant opposition forces along the battlefronts in the country. But where did the two groups get their cash and weapons? According to investigative reports, wealthy people from Saudi, Qatar, and Kuwait have been financing the radical groups, though these reports did not name the regimes of those countries as being involved because *"there was no clear evidence"* to this effect.

In November 2013, *The New York Times* ran a report that said huge amounts of money were being transferred from banks in Kuwait to support opposition fighters in Syria. Ghanim al-Mteiri, a Kuwaiti in charge of one the campaigns raising funds for the armed groups in Syria, told the NYT, *"Once upon a time we cooperated with the Americans in Iraq (in 1991). Now we want to get Bashar out of Syria, so why not cooperate with al-Qaeda?"*

"Qatari support for Syrian fighters"; "Wealthy Saudi and Kuwaiti sponsors"; "through banks in Kuwait": These revelations and more were mentioned repeatedly in most Western articles investigating the source of al-Nusra and ISIS funding, in addition to enumerating other sources such as seizure of weapons caches, robbing banks, and looting of other assets in Syria.

Recruitment for the "jihad" began in earnest, overtly and through the Internet, using religious and material inducements, with logistical facilities on the border. The radical jihadi monster thus grew in plain sight of everyone. In the meantime, Bandar was lobbying U.S. representatives and senators to support a US military strike on Syria. Bandar's self-confidence reached such an extent that he started criticizing Barack Obama's Syria policy publically.

Syria was drowning in weapons but the American military strike never came. Bandar was removed from his post at the helm of Saudi intelligence and the Syrian file in February 2014. US officials and analysts came out to say that a new less extreme Saudi phase would begin in Syria, and that Bandar had "gone too far" in supporting Syrian fighters. What does "too far" mean in this context? No one has yet explained it. Bandar's involvement in Syria and the region was stopped. But the ISIS monster had already become bigger, stronger, and richer. In June 2014, ISIS formalized this by declaring itself a state, not only in Syria, but also in Iraq.

## Bandar Bin Sultan

Prince Bandar bin Sultan, one-time long-serving ambassador to the United States, later head of Saudi intelligence, now adviser and special envoy to the king as well as secretary-general of the Saudi National Security Council (NSC).

Bandar fell out with the Obama Administration in 2012-2014 over the question of support for opposition fighters in Syria whom he wanted to back enthusiastically despite U.S. objections. Because of this, the White House came to view him as out of control and refused to work with him. Eventually, in April 2014, clearly responding to U.S. pressure, the king sacked him as intelligence chief but allowed him to keep his nebulous Saudi NSC role. Three months later, Bandar was back in favor in Riyadh, taking a special envoy role and has been seen at several top-level meetings since.

Saudi Arabia regards itself as the leader of the Muslim world, and as such sees itself as existing in an existential struggle with Iran for dominance of this world. The centuries old Sunni/Shiite divide, which has opened up dangerously since the 1979 Iranian revolution, is compounded by the political Islam of the Brotherhood, which views Arab monarchies such as the House of Saud as anachronisms at best but, more dangerously, un-Islamic.

For its part, Washington's principal interest in Saudi Arabia is safeguarding its role as the world's largest exporter of oil, with subsidiary interests of allowing Saudi Arabia to use market leverage to keep prices stable and not too high. This policy approach—which prompted U.S. military involvement after Saddam Hussein's 1990 invasion of Kuwait and explains the continuing naval and air force commitments in the Gulf area, though Saudi Arabia does not host any U.S. bases—tolerates (for the most part) often extraordinary behavior by the Saudis in their attempts to preserve what they regard as their Islamic pre-eminence.

Certainly in the past this has included support for terrorism. A particularly outrageous example of this: From about 1996 to around 2003, Defense Minister Prince Sultan and Interior Minister Prince Nayef paid off Osama bin Laden so al Qaeda would not target the kingdom.

Today, the Saudis deny any support for terrorists and, indeed, have made it a criminal offense for its citizens to fight in Syria or to provide support for opposiition fighters. But this is at odds with decades of Saudi practice, sending religious youth to fight in Afghanistan, Chechnya, Bosnia, and elsewhere. It is also not the way Bandar spoke of his instructions from King Abdullah when he was appointed intelligence chief: he stated that he was charged with getting rid of Bashar al Assad, containing Hezbollah in Lebanon, and cutting off the head of the snake (Iran). For emphasis of Saudi sincerity of purpose in Syria, he said that he would follow his monarch's instructions, even if it meant hiring "every SOB jihadist" he could find.

In policy circles in Washington, there is a common wisdom that Saudi support for fighters in Syria has not included al Qaeda types—though it's pretty obvious that Qatar, the kingdom's small neighbor but big diplomatic competitor has been supporting fighters of an al Qaeda affiliate (Jabhat al-Nusra).

In reality, the spectrum of opposition fighters—from President Obama's "teachers and pharmacists" through to IS, ISIS, ISIL (call it what you will)—is full of muddy distinctions. This could explain why Jordan, sandwiched between Saudi Arabia and Syria, declined to allow Bandar to set up training camps for hundreds, perhaps thousands, of opposition fighters. Jihadi types might influence disaffected Jordanian youth and would certainly annoy Assad, who could orchestrate a refugee crisis that might overwhelm Jordan. King Abdullah of Saudi Arabia was evidently so annoyed at the veto that he cut off all aid to cash-strapped Jordan this year, which had been running at $1 billion annually.

Despite the diplomacy which suggests an emerging coalition that includes Saudi Arabia and will take on the fighters of the Islamic State in Iraq and perhaps Syria, the House of Saud will likely continue to try to balance the threat of the head-chopping jihadists, while also trying to deliver a strategic setback to Iran by overthrowing the regime in Damascus.

From a Saudi point of view, the move of IS forces into Iraq contributed the removal of Nouri al-Maliki in Baghdad, who they regarded as a stooge of Tehran. Despite official support by Riyadh for the new Baghdad government, many Saudis who despise Shiites probably regard IS as doing God's work.

Saudi Arabia has denied giving any support to the Islamic State of Iraq and the Levant (Isis), the jihadi group that has captured swaths of territory across northern and central Iraq, as well as controlling large parts of northern Syria.

Stung by accusations from the Iraqi prime minister, Nouri al-Maliki, the normally reticent Saudi government issued a statement rejecting what it called "false allegations" and a "malicious falsehood".

Maliki claimed in a statement on Tuesday that the Saudis were facilitating genocide. Riyadh hit back by blaming Maliki's "exclusionary policies" for fomenting the crisis – a reference to the Shia politician's widely criticised sectarianism vis-a-vis Iraq's Sunni minority.

The Saudi monarchy has been a vocal supporter of the overthrow of the Syrian president, Bashar al-Assad, and sent money and weapons to rebel groups fighting against him from early on in the Syrian uprising. It has also called repeatedly for western arms – including anti-tank and anti-aircraft weapons – to be given to Syrian rebels "to level the playing-field" in the war.

Wealthy individuals and religious foundations in Saudi Arabia, Kuwait, Qatar and elsewhere in the Gulf have channelled millions of dollars to the anti-Assad opposition, though it is not clear with what degree of official connivance.

But since last autumn the Saudi government has diverted its support to a broad Islamic Front which has been fighting against jihadi formations such as Isis and the Syrian group Jabhat al-Nusra. There is other evidence of a rethink in the replacement of the Saudi intelligence chief, Prince Bandar bin Sultan, with Prince Mohamed bin Nayef, the interior minister and architect of a successful campaign against al-Qaida. The Saudis are also co-ordinating more closely with the US than previously. "*There is Saudi money flowing into Isis but it is not from the Saudi state,*" said Lina Khatib of the Carnegie Foundation.

The fear in Saudi Arabia is of an Afghan-style "blowback" of returning jihadis. It is similar to the concern of the UK and other western governments which are increasingly pre-occupied by a counter-terrorist agenda as they struggle to contain the effect of wars in Syria and Iraq that have merged into one and allowed Isis to claim that it is on the way to creating an Islamic emirate.

"*The Saudis have made many mistakes but I don't think support for Isis has been one of them,*" said Shashank Joshi, of the Royal United Services Institution. "*The kingdom recognizes the severity of the threat that Isis poses, particularly in the last few months. Private donations from Saudi and other Gulf states have probably been directed to Isis and those nations have generally been lax about monitoring those flows. Groups that Saudi Arabia has knowingly supported may have bled equipment, arms and funding to Isis but I don't think Riyadh had any real intention to support Isis as a counterweight to Assad or to Iran. They have been burned by Isis's jihadi forerunners. This is not to exculpate them for their carelessness. Maliki is trying to shift blame from himself and is echoing Iranian propaganda.*"

The Saudi statement said:"*The Kingdom of Saudi Arabia wishes to see the defeat and destruction of all al-Qaida networks and the Islamic State of Iraq and al-Sham (Isis) operating in Iraq. Saudi Arabia does not provide either moral or financial support to Isis or any terrorist networks.*"

# ISRAEL's
# GREAT MIDDLE EAST PROJECT

Longstanding neocon dreams to partition Iraq into three along ethnic and religious lines have been resurrected. White House officials now estimate that the fight against the region's 'Islamic State' will last years, and may outlive the Obama administration.

But this 'long war' vision goes back to nebulous ideas formally presented by late RAND Corp analyst Laurent Muraweic before the Pentagon's Defense Policy Board at the invitation of then chairman Richard Perle. That presentation described Iraq as a "tactical pivot" by which to transform the wider Middle East.

Brian Whitaker, former Guardian Middle East editor, rightly noted that the Perle-RAND strategy drew inspiration from a 1996 paper published by the Israeli Institute for Advanced Strategic and Political Studies, co-authored by Perle and other neocons who held top positions in the post-9/11 Bush administration.

The policy paper advocated a strategy that bears startling resemblance to the chaos unfolding in the wake of the expansion of the 'Islamic State' – Israel would "shape its strategic environment" by first securing the removal of Saddam Hussein. "Jordan and Turkey would form an axis along with Israel to weaken and 'roll back' Syria." This axis would attempt to weaken the influence of Lebanon, Syria and Iran by "weaning" off their Shi'ite populations. To succeed, Israel would need to engender US support, which would be obtained by Benjamin Netanyahu formulating the strategy "in language familiar to the Americans by tapping into themes of American administrations during the cold war."

The 2002 Perle-RAND plan was active in the Bush administration's strategic thinking on Iraq shortly before the 2003 war. According to US private intelligence firm Stratfor, in late 2002, then vice-president Dick Cheney and deputy defense secretary Paul Wolfowitz had co-authored a scheme under which central Sunni-majority Iraq would join with Jordan; the northern Kurdish regions would become an autonomous state; all becoming separate from the southern Shi'ite region.

The strategic advantages of an Iraq partition, Stratfor argued, focused on US control of oil: The expansion of the 'Islamic State' has provided a pretext for the fundamental contours of this scenario to unfold, with the US and British looking to re-establish a long-term military presence in Iraq in the name of the "defense of a young new state."

In 2006, Cheney's successor, Joe Biden, also indicated his support for the 'soft partition' of Iraq along ethno-religious lines – a position which the co-author of the Biden-Iraq plan, Leslie Gelb of the Council on Foreign Relations, now argues is "the only solution" to the current crisis.

Also in 2006, the Armed Forces Journal published a map of the Middle East with its borders thoroughly re-drawn, courtesy of Lt. Col. (ret.) Ralph Peters, who had previously been assigned to the Office of the Deputy Chief of Staff for Intelligence where he was responsible for future warfare. As for the goals of this plan, apart from "security from terrorism" and "the prospect of democracy", Peters also mentioned "access to oil supplies in a region that is destined to fight itself."

In 2008, the strategy re-surfaced – once again via RAND Corp – through a report funded by the US Army Training and Doctrine Command on how to prosecute the 'long war.' Among its strategies, one scenario advocated by the report was 'Divide and Rule' which would involve:

## The Sionist strategy

Almost thirty years ago, a prominent group of neoconservative hawks found an effective vehicle for advocating their views via the Committee on the Present Danger, a group that fervently believed the United States was a hair away from being militarily surpassed by the Soviet Union, and whose raison d'être was strident advocacy of bigger military budgets, near-fanatical opposition to any form of arms control and zealous championing of a Likudnik Israel. Considered a marginal group in its nascent days during the Carter Administration, with the election of Ronald Reagan in 1980 CPD went from the margins to the center of power.

Just as the right-wing defense intellectuals made CPD a cornerstone of a shadow defense establishment during the Carter Administration, so, too, did the right during the Clinton years, in part through two organizations: the Jewish Institute for National Security Affairs (JINSA) and the Center for Security Policy (CSP). And just as was the case two decades ago, dozens of their members have ascended to powerful government posts, where their advocacy in support of the same agenda continues, abetted by the out-of-government adjuncts from which they came.

Industrious and persistent, they've managed to weave a number of issues--support for national missile defense, opposition to arms control treaties, championing of wasteful weapons systems, arms aid to Turkey and American unilateralism in general--into a hard line, with support for the Israeli right at its core.

On no issue is the JINSA/CSP hard line more evident than in its relentless campaign for war-- not just with Iraq, but "total war," as Michael Ledeen, one of the most influential JINSAns in Washington, put it last year. For this crew, "regime change" by any means necessary in Iraq, Iran, Syria, Saudi Arabia and the Palestinian Authority is an urgent imperative. Anyone who dissents--be it Colin Powell's State Department, the CIA or career military officers--is committing heresy against articles of faith that effectively hold there is no difference between US and Israeli national security interests, and that the only way to assure continued safety and prosperity for both countries is through hegemony in the Middle East--a hegemony achieved with the traditional cold war recipe of feints, force, clientism and covert action.

For example, the Pentagon's Defense Policy Board--chaired by JINSA/CSP adviser and former Reagan Administration Defense Department official Richard Perle, and stacked with advisers from both groups--recently made news by listening to a briefing that cast Saudi Arabia as an enemy to be brought to heel through a number of potential mechanisms, many of which mirror JINSA's recommendations, and which reflect the JINSA/CSP crowd's preoccupation with Egypt. (The final slide of the Defense Policy Board presentation proposed that "Grand Strategy for the Middle East" should concentrate on "Iraq as the tactical pivot, Saudi Arabia as the strategic pivot [and] Egypt as the prize.")

Ledeen has been leading the charge for regime change in Iran, while old comrades like Andrew Marshall and Harold Rhode in the Pentagon's Office of Net Assessment actively tinker with ways to re-engineer both the Iranian and Saudi governments. JINSA is also cheering the US military on as it tries to secure basing rights in the strategic Red Sea country of Eritrea, happily failing to mention that the once-promising secular regime of President Isaiais Afewerki continues to slide into the kind of repressive authoritarianism practiced by the "axis of evil" and its adjuncts.

Indeed, there are some in military and intelligence circles who have taken to using "axis of evil" in reference to JINSA and CSP, along with venerable repositories of hawkish thinking like the American Enterprise Institute and the Hudson Institute, as well as defense contractors, conservative foundations and public relations entities underwritten by far-right American Zionists (all of which help to underwrite JINSA and CSP).

It's a milieu where ideology and money seamlessly blend: "Whenever you see someone identified in print or on TV as being with the Center for Security Policy or JINSA championing a position on the grounds of ideology or principle--which they are unquestionably doing with conviction--you are, nonetheless, not informed that they're also providing a sort of cover for other ideologues who just happen to stand to profit from hewing to the Likudnik and Pax Americana lines," says a veteran intelligence officer.

## JINSA / CSP

Founded in 1976 by neoconservatives concerned that the United States might not be able to provide Israel with adequate military supplies in the event of another Arab-Israeli war, over the past twenty-five years JINSA has gone from a loose-knit proto-group to a $1.4-million-a-year operation with a formidable array of Washington power players on its rolls.

Until the beginning of the previous Bush Administration, JINSA's board of advisers included such heavy hitters as Dick Cheney, John Bolton and Douglas Feith, the third-highest-ranking executive in the Pentagon during W. Bush administration. Both Perle and former Director of Central Intelligence James Woolsey, two of the loudest voices in the attack-Iraq chorus, are still on the board, as are such Reagan-era relics as Jeane Kirkpatrick, Eugene Rostow and Ledeen--Oliver North's Iran/*contra* liaison with the Israelis.

According to its website, JINSA exists to "educate the American public about the importance of an effective US defense capability so that our vital interests as Americans can be safeguarded" and to "inform the American defense and foreign affairs community about the important role Israel can and does play in bolstering democratic interests in the Mediterranean and the Middle East." In practice, this translates into its members producing a steady stream of op-eds and reports that have been good indicators of what the Pentagon's civilian leadership is thinking.

JINSA relishes denouncing virtually any type of contact between the US government and Syria and finding new ways to demonize the Palestinians. To give but one example (and one that kills two birds with one stone): According to JINSA, not only is Yasir Arafat in control of all violence in the occupied territories, but he orchestrates the violence solely "to protect Saddam.... Saddam is at the moment Arafat's only real financial supporter.... [Arafat] has no incentive to stop the violence against Israel and allow the West to turn its attention to his mentor and paymaster."

And if there's a way to advance other aspects of the far-right agenda by intertwining them with Israeli interests, JINSA doesn't hesitate there, either. A recent report contends that the Arctic National Wildlife Refuge must be tapped because "the Arab oil-producing states" are countries "with interests inimical to ours," but Israel "stand[s] with us when we need [Israel]," and a US policy of tapping oil under ANWR will "limit [the Arabs'] ability to do damage to either of us."

The bulk of JINSA's modest annual budget is spent on taking a bevy of retired US generals and admirals to Israel, where JINSA facilitates meetings between Israeli officials and the still-influential US flag officers, who, upon their return to the States, happily write op-eds and sign letters and advertisements championing the Likudnik line. (Sowing seeds for the future, JINSA also takes US service academy cadets to Israel each summer and sponsors a lecture series at the Army, Navy and Air Force academies.)

In one such statement, issued soon after the outbreak of the latest intifada, twenty-six JINSAns of retired flag rank, including many from the advisory board, struck a moralizing tone, characterizing Palestinian violence as a "perversion of military ethics" and holding that "America's role as facilitator in this process should never yield to America's responsibility as a friend to Israel," as "friends don't leave friends on the battlefield."

However high-minded this might sound, the post service associations of the letter's signatories--which are almost always left off the organization's website and communiqués--ought to require that the phrase be amended to say "friends don't leave friends on the battlefield, especially when there's business to be done and bucks to be made." Almost every retired officer who sits on JINSA's board of advisers or has participated in its Israel trips or signed a JINSA letter works or has worked with military contractors who do business with the Pentagon and Israel.

While some keep a low profile as self-employed "consultants" and avoid mention of their clients, others are less shy about their associations, including with the private mercenary firm Military Professional Resources International, weapons broker and military consultancy Cypress International and SY Technology, whose main clients include the Pentagon's Missile Defense Agency, which oversees several ongoing joint projects with Israel.

## Military-Industrial Complex

The behemoths of military contracting are also well represented in JINSA's ranks. For example, JINSA advisory board members Adm. Leon Edney, Adm. David Jeremiah and Lieut. Gen. Charles May, all retired, have served Northrop Grumman or its subsidiaries as either consultants or board members. Northrop Grumman has built ships for the Israeli Navy and sold F-16 avionics and E-2C Hawkeye planes to the Israeli Air Force (as well as the Longbow radar system to the Israeli army for use in its attack helicopters).

It also works with Tamam, a subsidiary of Israeli Aircraft Industries, to produce an unmanned aerial vehicle. Lockheed Martin has sold more than $2 billion worth of F-16s to Israel since 1999, as well as flight simulators, multiple-launch rocket systems and Seahawk heavyweight torpedoes. At one time or another, General May, retired Lieut. Gen. Paul Cerjan and retired Adm. Carlisle Trost have labored in LockMart's vineyards. Trost has also sat on the board of General Dynamics, whose Gulfstream subsidiary has a $206 million contract to supply planes to Israel to be used for "special electronics missions."

By far the most profitably diversified of the JINSAns is retired Adm. David Jeremiah. President and partner of Technology Strategies & Alliances Corporation (described as a "strategic advisory firm and investment banking firm engaged primarily in the aerospace, defense, telecommunications and electronics industries"), Jeremiah also sits on the boards of Northrop Grumman's Litton subsidiary and of defense giant Alliant Techsystems, which--in partnership with Israel's TAAS--does a brisk business in rubber bullets. And he had a seat on the Pentagon's Defense Policy Board, chaired by Perle.

About the only major defense contractor without a presence on JINSA's advisory board is Boeing, which has had a relationship with Israeli Aircraft Industries for thirty years. (Boeing also sells F-15s to Israel and, in partnership with Lockheed Martin, Apache attack helicopters, a ubiquitous weapon in the occupied territories.)

But take a look at JINSA's kindred spirit in things pro-Likud and pro-Star Wars, the Center for Security Policy, and there on its national security advisory council are Stanley Ebner, a former Boeing executive; Andrew Ellis, vice president for government relations; and Carl Smith, a former staff director of the Senate Armed Services Committee who, as a lawyer in private practice, has counted Boeing among his clients. "JINSA and CSP," says a veteran Pentagon analyst, "may as well be one and the same."

Not a hard sell: There's always been considerable overlap beween the JINSA and CSP rosters--JINSA advisers Jeane Kirkpatrick, Richard Perle and Phyllis Kaminsky also served on CSP's advisory council; current JINSA advisory board chairman David Steinmann sits on CSP's board of directors; and before returning to the Pentagon Douglas Feith served as the board's chair. At this writing, twenty-two CSP advisers--including additional Reagan-era remnants like Elliott Abrams, Ken deGraffenreid, Paula Dobriansky, Sven Kraemer, Robert Joseph, Robert

Andrews and J.D. Crouch--have reoccupied key positions in the national security establishment, as have other true believers of more recent vintage.

While CSP boasts an impressive advisory list of hawkish luminaries, its star is Frank Gaffney, its founder, president and CEO. A protégé of Perle going back to their days as staffers for the late Senator Henry "Scoop" Jackson (*a k a* the Senator from Boeing, and the Senate's most zealous champion of Israel in his day), Gaffney later joined Perle at the Pentagon, only to be shown the door by Defense Secretary Frank Carlucci in 1987, not long after Perle left.

Gaffney then reconstituted the latest incarnation of the Committee on the Present Danger. Beyond compiling an A-list of influential conservative hawks, Gaffney has been prolific over the past fifteen years, churning out a constant stream of reports (as well as regular columns for the *Washington Times*) making the case that the gravest threats to US national security are China, Iraq, still-undeveloped ballistic missiles launched by rogue states, and the passage of or adherence to virtually any form of arms control treaty.

Gaffney and CSP's prescriptions for national security have been fairly simple: Gut all arms control treaties, push ahead with weapons systems virtually everyone agrees should be killed (such as the V-22 Osprey), give no quarter to the Palestinians and, most important, go full steam ahead on just about every national missile defense program. (CSP was heavily represented on the late-1990s Commission to Assess the Ballistic Missile Threat to the United States, which was instrumental in keeping the program alive during the Clinton years.)

Looking at the center's affiliates, it's not hard to see why: Not only are makers of the Osprey (Boeing) well represented on the CSP's board of advisers but so too is Lockheed Martin (by vice president for space and strategic missiles Charles Kupperman and director of defense systems Douglas Graham). Former TRW executive Amoretta Hoeber is also a CSP adviser, as is former Congressman and Raytheon lobbyist Robert Livingston. Ball Aerospace & Technologies--a major manufacturer of NASA and Pentagon satellites--is represented by former Navy Secretary John Lehman, while missile-defense computer systems maker Hewlett-Packard is represented by George Keyworth, who is on its board of directors. And the Congressional Missile Defense Caucus and Osprey (or "tilt rotor") caucus are represented by Representative Curt Weldon and Senator Jon Kyl.

CSP was instrumental in developing the arguments against the Anti-Ballistic Missile Treaty. Largely ignored or derided at the time, a 1995 CSP memo co-written by Douglas Feith holding that the United States should withdraw from the ABM treaty has essentially become policy, as have other CSP reports opposing the Comprehensive Test Ban Treaty, the Chemical Weapons Convention and the International Criminal Court.

## A Clean Break

But perhaps the most insightful window on the JINSA/CSP policy worldview comes in the form of a paper Perle and Feith collaborated on in 1996 with six others under the auspices of the Institute for Advanced Strategic and Political Studies. Essentially an advice letter to ascendant Israeli politician Benjamin Netanyahu, "A Clean Break: A New Strategy for

Securing the Realm" makes for insightful reading as a kind of US-Israeli neoconservative manifesto.

The paper's first prescription was for an Israeli rightward economic shift, with tax cuts and a selloff of public lands and enterprises--moves that would also engender support from a "broad bipartisan spectrum of key pro-Israeli Congressional leaders." But beyond economics, the paper essentially reads like a blueprint for a mini-cold war in the Middle East, advocating the use of proxy armies for regime changes, destabilization and containment.

Indeed, it even goes so far as to articulate a way to advance right-wing Zionism by melding it with missile-defense advocacy. "Mr. Netanyahu can highlight his desire to cooperate more closely with the United States on anti-missile defense in order to remove the threat of blackmail which even a weak and distant army can pose to either state," it reads. "Not only would such cooperation on missile defense counter a tangible physical threat to Israel's survival, but it would broaden Israel's base of support among many in the United States Congress who may know little about Israel, but care very much about missile defense"-- something that has the added benefit of being "helpful in the effort to move the US embassy in Israel to Jerusalem."

Though the general agenda put forth by JINSA and CSP continues to be reflected in councils of war, even some of the hawks (including Rumsfeld deputy Paul Wolfowitz) are growing increasingly leery of Israel's settlements policy and Gaffney's relentless support for it. Indeed, his personal stock in Bush Administration circles is low. "Gaffney has worn out his welcome by being an overbearing gadfly rather than a serious contributor to policy," says a senior Pentagon political official. Since earlier this year, White House political adviser Karl Rove has been casting about for someone to start a new, more mainstream defense group that would counter the influence of CSP. According to those who have communicated with Rove on the matter, his quiet efforts are in response to complaints from many conservative activists who feel let down by Gaffney, or feel he's too hard on President Bush. "A lot of us have taken [Gaffney] at face value over the years," one influential conservative says. "Yet we now know he's pushed for some of the most flawed missile defense and conventional systems. He considered Cuba a 'classic asymmetric threat' but not Al Qaeda. And since 9/11, he's been less concerned with the threat to America than to Israel."

## ISIS and Israel

Why is IS – formerly known as the Islamic State in Iraq and Syria (ISIS) – not fighting Israel? Would anything change if its fighters were to gain access to the borders with occupied Palestine?

While the Israeli military machine was massacring people in Gaza – and amid the euphoria among some jihadis over the news of the announcement of an "Islamic caliphate" – video footage of masked individuals firing rockets into Israel was posted online, and attributed to IS. Many cheered for what they saw as the "Muslim caliph's" response to calls for succor from the people of Gaza, even believing the "caliphate" was very close to liberating Jerusalem. But the euphoria did not last very long.

The video turned out to be from an old footage dating back to 2012, recorded by the militant group known as the Mujahideen Shura Council, and was repurposed to be attributed to IS. IS-affiliated social media activists such as Turujman al-Asawirti were also quick to question the authenticity of the video attributed to their group.

*Al-Akhbar* had a number of questions for IS supporters from Lebanon, Syria, and Iraq, including the following: Why has IS maintained its distance from the events in Palestine? Are the people of Gaza not Muslims after all? Does this posture not reinforce the premise that there is a hidden link between Zionism and Salafi-Jihadism that appeases Israel, or is geography alone to blame for their inaction?

In a speech by IS leader Abu Bakr al-Baghdadi, after he installed himself as caliph of the Muslims, he spoke about the terror inflicted on Palestine, but he did so only in passing, in the wider context of the terror Muslims face around the world.

In substance, they believe that liberating Palestine is irrelevant without the establishment of the caliphate in the countries surrounding Palestine first. Before him, in the time of the late leader of al-Qaeda Osama bin Laden, the jihadi attitude on Palestine was also controversial. Why have the jihadis never declared Palestine an arena for their jihad?

In effect, the leader of global jihadism Sheikh Ayman al-Zawahiri had an interesting position, approaching the issue from the angle of priorities on the basis of "Dar al-Kufr and Dar al-Islam," or the abode of disbelief and the abode of belief in jihadi lore. Zawahiri argues that fighting in Palestine should be on the basis that it is an abode of Islam, and that therefore, liberating it is a duty for every Muslim, as stated in his speech "truths about the conflict between Islam and infidelity" in 2007. But despite this, Palestine remains at the bottom of the list of priorities for most jihadis.

In form, most adherents of Salafi-Jihadism believe that "Shias are more dangerous than Jews." In substance, they believe that liberating Palestine is irrelevant without the establishment of the caliphate in the countries surrounding Palestine first.
Sources linked to IS told *Al-Akhbar*, "The final war that will liberate Palestine will be led by the caliphate, preceded by the establishment of this state in the Levant and Iraq," on the basis of sayings they attribute to Prophet Mohammad. The sources add, "Allah alone knows just how much the soldiers of the caliphate yearn for skipping the necessary stages and battle the Jews in Palestine, but he who rushes something before its time comes shall be punished by being denied it."

The sources, who are based in the Raqqa province of Syria, enumerate these necessary stages, saying, "The priority is to liberate Baghdad, then head to Damascus and liberate all of the Levant, before liberating Palestine."

This is the principle that IS soldiers follow: "Fighting nearby apostates is more important than fighting faraway infidels." To justify this, they rely on the Wars of Apostasy initiated by the Caliph Abu Bakr (against Muslims who renounced their religion following the death of the Prophet), who made it a priority over fighting infidels and Muslim conquests.

According to IS fighters, the adherents of all Islamic sects who do not submit to their "caliph" are either "apostates or misguided folk, who should be fought and killed, forced to repent and let themselves be guided, or be liberated from apostate rule." A jihadi adds here, "We the followers of this path follow sharia not the whims of men," adding that the Prophet had fought Quraysh first before moving on to fight the Jews of Banu Qurayza.

These sharia-based arguments are "reinforced" by the reality on the ground. A jihadi argues, "No one can initiate a battle against Israel except through the [direct] borders." The jihadi then adds sarcastically, "Certainly, the mujahideen will not be able to bomb Israel by air," before he said, "IS is still far from Israel. If it reaches Jordan and southern Syria (the Golan and Quneitra), then things would be different."

The jihadis base their vision on their perception that "Syria, Lebanon, Egypt, and Jordan all collaborate with Israel," and argue that any attack they initiate would be stopped by what they call the "idolatry" regimes in the name of security. A jihadi opines, "Since the countries adjacent to Israel do not fire a single bullet at it, this means they do not want a confrontation with Israel. Any attempt to use their territories to target Israel means automatically a confrontation with these regimes. Therefore, we must first purge these countries to get to Israel."

The IS-affiliated jihadis conclude that "the enmity the Arab countries and Arab groups have with Israel are in words not deeds, that is, only in politics and slogans. As long as this is the case, any group that wants to operate will confront these regimes." As proof of their point, the jihadis give the example of the Abdullah Azzam Brigades' operations out of South Lebanon, and the subsequent crackdown on the group's members after they fired rockets into Israel. For this reason, these jihadis believe that the priority is for their "state" to expand gradually, and that everything else is meaningless and illogical.

With regards to suicide operations, the jihadis said, "This is on the table, but the time for it has not yet come."